ABC | ABC

delicious.

Spice

Welcome

Spices are at the heart of some of my favourite dishes.
I love the way the same spice used in a different dish
can take your cooking to a completely new place.

Spice brings the colour, heat and aroma of some of the
most beautiful and exotic places in the world right to your
table, so whether you want to be transported to Thailand for
beef curry, or Morocco for fish with chermoula, it's all here
in a celebration of the diversity of modern Australian cooking.

We've gathered 60 of our favourite dishes, from fast
stir-fries and Asian salads to slow-cooked Indian curries, with
each recipe designed to make it easy for you to create
maximum flavour.

Happy cooking!

Valli

Contents

Beef and Lamb

Vegetarian

Crab and corn cakes with coriander dipping sauce

1 egg
⅓ cup (50g) plain flour
1 garlic clove, finely chopped
Stems of 4 coriander sprigs,
    roughly chopped
Kernels cut from 3 fresh
    corn cobs
200g fresh crabmeat*
2 spring onions, thinly sliced
Sunflower oil, to deep-fry
Lime wedges, to serve

Coriander dipping sauce
½ cup (110g) caster sugar
¼ cup (60ml) rice vinegar
1 tbs fish sauce
1 tbs sweet chilli sauce
2 small red chillies, finely
    chopped
2 tbs coriander leaves, finely
    chopped

For the dipping sauce, place the sugar in a saucepan with the vinegar and ¼ cup (60ml) water, then stir over low heat until the sugar dissolves. Cool slightly, then add the fish sauce, sweet chilli sauce, fresh chilli and chopped coriander leaves. Set aside the dipping sauce until needed.

Place the egg, flour, garlic, coriander stems and one-third of the corn in a food processor and process to a rough paste. Add the crabmeat and spring onion, then pulse briefly to just combine. Transfer to a bowl, then mix with the remaining corn kernels and season well with salt and pepper.

Half-fill a deep-fryer or large saucepan with the oil and heat to 190°C (a cube of bread will turn golden in 30 seconds when the oil is hot enough). Working in batches, carefully drop a heaped tablespoon of batter into the oil for each fritter. Fry, turning, for 1–2 minutes until golden and crisp. Remove using a slotted spoon and drain on paper towel. Repeat to make 12 fritters in total. Serve immediately with the coriander dipping sauce and lime wedges.
Makes 12

* Fresh crabmeat is available from fishmongers.

Quail eggs with walnut hummus and dukkah

½ cup (60g) chopped
   toasted walnuts
250g tub hummus
2 tbs sour cream
1 tbs chopped flat-leaf
   parsley
12 quail eggs*
Roasted cherry truss
   tomatoes and warm pita
   bread, to serve
Walnut oil* or olive oil,
   to drizzle
½ cup dukkah*
Mint leaves, to garnish

Place the walnuts in a food processor and pulse to form fine crumbs. Add the hummus, sour cream and parsley, then pulse to combine.

Place the eggs in a saucepan of cold water and bring to the boil, then boil for 4 minutes. Peel the eggs under cold running water while still warm.

Place the hummus mixture and eggs on a serving plate with the cherry tomatoes. Drizzle with the oil and sprinkle with the dukkah. Garnish with the mint and serve with the warm pita. **Serves 4 as a starter or to share**

* Quail eggs are from selected poultry shops and delis. Dukkah (a spice, nut and seed blend) and walnut oil are from delis and gourmet shops.

Spicy fishcakes with pickled-ginger mayonnaise

300g hot-smoked salmon*
   or trout*
2 cups (about 400g) mashed
   potato, cooled completely
4 spring onions, thinly sliced
1 tbs Thai green curry paste
1 small red chilli, seeds
   removed, finely chopped
2 tbs finely chopped
   coriander
1 egg, lightly beaten
½ cup (75g) plain flour
Sunflower oil, to shallow-fry
Pickled ginger and
   lemon wedges, to serve

Pickled-ginger mayonnaise
½ cup (150g) mayonnaise
   (preferably Japanese*)
2 tbs chopped pickled ginger,
   plus 1 tbs pickling juice

Remove the skin and any bones from the fish and flake into small pieces. Place the fish in a bowl with the potato, spring onion, curry paste, chilli, coriander and egg. Season well and then mix with a fork until combined. Divide the mixture into 6 portions, then use damp hands to mould into patties. Chill for 30 minutes or until firm.

Meanwhile, for the pickled ginger mayonnaise, combine the mayonnaise, pickled ginger and pickling juice in a bowl. Cover and keep chilled until ready to serve.

Place the flour in a shallow bowl and season. Coat the fishcakes in the flour, shaking off any excess. Heat 3cm of the oil in a large frypan over medium heat. Fry the fishcakes for 2 minutes each side or until golden and crisp.

Season the fishcakes and serve with the pickled-ginger mayonnaise, pickled ginger and lemon wedges. **Makes 6**

* Hot-smoked salmon, hot-smoked trout and Japanese mayonnaise are available from supermarkets and gourmet food shops.

Prawn cakes on lemongrass skewers

2 eschalots, finely chopped

2 tbs Thai green curry paste

1 small red chilli, seeds
  removed, finely chopped

1 tsp grated ginger

2 tsp fish sauce

1 tbs light soy sauce

¼ cup chopped coriander

300g skinless, boneless white
  fish fillets (such as ling)

200g green prawn meat

1 eggwhite

2 tbs plain flour

5 lemongrass stems, cut into
  ten 15cm pieces (optional)

Sunflower oil, to shallow-fry

Lime wedges, to serve

Green papaya salad

1 long red chilli, seeds
  removed, finely chopped

2 cloves garlic, chopped

2 tbs grated palm sugar*

Juice of 1 lime

1 tbs tamarind concentrate*

2 tbs fish sauce

3 cups shredded green
  papaya

¼ cup each chopped
  coriander and mint

To make the green papaya salad, place the chilli, garlic and sugar in a mortar and pestle and pound to a smooth paste. Stir in the lime juice, tamarind and fish sauce. Toss in a bowl with the papaya and herbs. Mix well.

Place the eschalot, curry paste, chilli, ginger, fish sauce, soy sauce and coriander in a food processor and pulse until combined. Add the fish, prawn meat, eggwhite and flour, season with salt and pepper and pulse until the mixture comes together.

Using damp hands, roll the mixture into 10 small cakes. Use your hand to flatten slightly, then mould each cake around a lemongrass piece if using, or leave as patties. Chill in the fridge to firm up.

Heat 3–4cm of the oil in a frypan over medium-low heat. Cook the prawn cakes, in batches, for 2 minutes each side until golden. Drain on paper towel. Serve with the green papaya salad and lime wedges. **Makes 10**

* Available from Asian food shops.

Sushi stacks

125g short-grain sushi rice*

1½ tbs rice vinegar

1 tsp caster sugar

1 tsp wasabi paste*, plus
   extra to serve

1½ tsp finely grated ginger

1 tbs lime juice

350g sashimi-grade salmon,
   pin-boned, cut into 1cm
   pieces

1 Lebanese cucumber, seeds
   removed, chopped

Black sesame seeds*,
   chopped chives, micro
   herbs or coriander and soy
   sauce, to serve

Rinse the rice under cold water until the water runs clear. Place the rice in a saucepan with 200ml cold water. Cover with a lid, bring to the boil, then reduce the heat to low and cook for 10 minutes. Remove from the heat and stand, covered, for 10 minutes or until the water is absorbed – don't be tempted to lift the lid early as you will lose the steam that cooks the rice. Combine the vinegar, sugar and ½ teaspoon salt in a small bowl, then stir into the rice. Allow to cool.

Stir the wasabi paste, ginger and lime juice together in a bowl. Add the salmon and cucumber, then toss gently to combine.

Place a 7cm x 3cm ring mould on each serving plate, then divide the rice mixture among the moulds. (Alternatively, place small mounds of rice on each plate.) Top with the salmon mixture, then remove the moulds, if using. Scatter with the sesame seeds and herbs, then serve immediately with soy sauce and extra wasabi.

Serves 6

* Sushi rice, wasabi paste and black sesame seeds are from selected supermarkets and Asian food shops. Sashimi-grade salmon is from fishmongers.

Pimientos de Padron

30–40 pimientos de Padron*
½ cup (125ml) extra virgin
 olive oil
Chargrilled bread, to serve

Wash the pimientos and pat dry. Heat the olive oil in a large frypan over medium heat. Add the pimientos and cook, turning, for 5–6 minutes until the skins blister and the peppers start to wilt. Sprinkle with sea salt, then serve warm with drinks, chargrilled bread and other tapas dishes, such as marinated anchovies and pan-fried chorizo, if desired. **Serves 6**

* From selected greengrocers or order from Queensland's Midyim Eco, midyimeco.com.au.

Potato 'tacos' with tomato salsa

8 desiree potatoes (unpeeled)
1 tbs olive oil
25g unsalted butter
½ tsp smoked paprika
  (pimenton)
Guacamole and sour cream,
  to serve

Tomato salsa
400g can chopped tomatoes
2 eschalots, chopped
100g brown sugar
⅓ cup (80ml) white wine
  vinegar
½ tsp smoked paprika
  (pimenton)

Guacamole
2 avocados, chopped
2 long red or green chillies,
  seeds removed, finely
  chopped
¼ cup coriander leaves,
  roughly chopped
1 garlic clove, crushed
1 tbs lime juice
1 tsp ground cumin

Preheat the oven to 200°C. Line a baking tray with baking paper. Prick the potatoes with a fork, then place on the baking tray and drizzle with the oil. Bake for 1–1½ hours until tender. Cool, halve, then scoop out and discard the soft potato centre, reserving the potato skins – these will become your 'taco' shells.

Meanwhile, for the tomato salsa, place all the ingredients in a saucepan and bring to the boil. Reduce the heat to low, season, then simmer, stirring occasionally, for 25–30 minutes until thick. Cool slightly.

Place the butter and paprika in a small saucepan over low heat and cook until melted and combined. Toss the potato skins in the paprika butter, then place, cut-side up, on a baking paper-lined baking tray and bake for a further 15 minutes or until crisp.

To make the guacamole, place the avocado, chilli, coriander, garlic, lime juice and cumin in a food processor and season with sea salt and freshly ground black pepper. Whiz until just combined, but not smooth – you want to keep some texture.

Serve the potato 'tacos' with the guacamole, sour cream and warm tomato salsa. **Serves 4**

Spicy bean soup with cumin puris

2 tbs olive oil

2 onions, finely chopped

450g carrots, cut into 2cm
  cubes

2 tsp grated ginger

1 tbs korma curry paste

1L (4 cups) chicken or
  vegetable stock

200ml coconut milk, plus
  extra to drizzle

Juice of 1 large lime

400g can cannellini beans,
  rinsed, drained

Toasted cumin seeds,
  to sprinkle

Cumin puris

100g wholemeal flour

100g plain flour, plus extra
  to dust

2 tbs sunflower oil, plus extra
  to shallow-fry

1½ tsp cumin seeds

For the puris, sift the flours and a pinch of salt into a bowl, then rub in the oil until the mixture resembles breadcrumbs. Stir in the cumin seeds, then gradually stir in 150ml water to make a soft, slightly sticky dough. Turn out onto a lightly floured surface and knead for 5 minutes until smooth. Form the dough into a ball, lightly coat with oil, then place in a bowl. Cover with plastic wrap and stand at room temperature for 15 minutes.

Divide the dough into 12 balls and dust heavily with flour. Roll each ball out to form a 13cm disc. Pour 1cm of the oil into a deep frypan over high heat and heat to 180°C or until a cube of bread turns golden brown in 30 seconds. One at a time, shallow-fry the puris for 45 seconds each side until puffed and golden, adding more oil if needed. Drain on paper towel. Keep warm in a low oven while you make the soup.

Meanwhile, heat the oil in a large saucepan over medium-low heat. Add the onion and cook, stirring, for 2–3 minutes until softened but not coloured. Add the carrot and ginger and cook for a further minute. Stir in the curry paste and cook for 30 seconds until fragrant. Add the stock and bring to the boil, then reduce the heat to medium–low and simmer for 8–10 minutes until the carrot is tender. Add the coconut milk, lime juice and beans and allow to simmer for a further 5 minutes. Blend with a hand blender (or cool slightly, then blend in batches in a blender) until smooth. Gently reheat over low heat. Divide the soup among serving bowls, drizzle with extra coconut milk, sprinkle with the cumin seeds, then serve with the cumin puris. **Serves 4–6**

Asian steak tartare with wonton crisps

8 wonton wrappers*
Sunflower oil, to shallow-fry
300g good-quality beef rump
    or eye-fillet steak, trimmed,
    very finely chopped
4 quail egg yolks*
Micro herbs* or extra
    coriander leaves and fried
    Asian shallots*, to serve

Dressing
2 tsp sunflower oil
1 tbs finely chopped
    coriander
1 tbs finely chopped
    Vietnamese* or regular
    mint
2 tbs fish sauce
2 tsp caster sugar
2 tsp finely grated lime zest
1½ tsp lime juice
2 tsp rice vinegar
1 tsp sriracha chilli sauce*
    or chilli jam*

Using scissors, cut the wonton wrappers in half on the diagonal. Heat 2cm of the oil in a small saucepan. In batches, shallow-fry the wonton wrapper halves for 30 seconds or until puffed and crisp. Drain the wonton crisps on paper towel. Set aside.

For the dressing, place all the ingredients in a bowl and whisk to combine. Taste, then adjust the flavours as needed – there should be a balance of salty, hot, sour and sweet.

Add the chopped steak to the dressing and mix well to combine. Place an egg ring on each serving plate, then divide the steak mixture among the egg rings. Make a small indent in the top of the steak mixture using the back of a teaspoon, then carefully place an egg yolk in each indent. Carefully remove the egg rings, then scatter with the herbs and fried shallots. Serve immediately with the wonton crisps. **Serves 4**

* Wonton wrappers, quail eggs, Vietnamese mint, sriracha chilli sauce and chilli jam are from Asian food shops. Micro herbs are from selected greengrocers and growers' markets.

Vegetable bhaji salad

250g besan (chickpea flour)*
1 tsp dried chilli flakes
1 tsp ground turmeric
1 tsp ground cumin
6 fresh curry leaves*, finely
 shredded
200g sour cream or creme
 fraiche
⅓ cup (80ml) lemon juice
1 large carrot, cut into thin
 matchsticks
50g eggplant, cut into thin
 matchsticks
100g snow peas,
 cut into thin strips
Sunflower oil, to deep-fry
Mesclun (mixed baby salad
 leaves) or micro herbs*,
 to serve

Combine the besan, chilli flakes, turmeric, cumin, ½ teaspoon salt and enough cold water to make a thickish batter, then stir through the curry leaves. Leave the batter to rest in the fridge for 15 minutes.

Combine the sour cream or creme fraiche with the lemon juice to make a loose dressing. Season with sea salt and freshly ground black pepper, then set aside.

Place the carrot, eggplant and snow peas in a bowl, then toss with the batter.

Half-fill a deep-fryer or large saucepan with the oil, then heat to 180°C (the oil is hot enough when a cube of bread turns golden in 30 seconds). Working in batches and using a heaped tablespoon of batter for each bhaji, drop spoonfuls into the oil and cook for 2 minutes each side, turning once, until golden and cooked through. Remove with a slotted spoon and drain on paper towel, then keep warm while you repeat with the remaining batter.

To serve, divide the salad leaves or herbs among 4 plates, top each with 2–3 bhaji, then sprinkle with salt and drizzle with the dressing. **Serves 4**

* Besan and fresh curry leaves are from Asian food shops and selected greengrocers. Micro herbs are from selected greengrocers and growers' markets.

Hummus soup

1L (4 cups) chicken stock

3 garlic cloves, finely
  chopped

Grated zest and juice of
  1 small lemon, plus wedges
  to serve

2 x 400g cans chickpeas,
  rinsed, drained

1 tbs chopped mint leaves

1 tbs chopped flat-leaf
  parsley leaves

Natural yoghurt, to drizzle

Extra virgin olive oil, to
  drizzle

2 tbs dukkah*

Flatbread, to serve

Place the stock in a saucepan with the garlic, lemon zest and
chickpeas and bring to the boil over medium-high heat. Reduce the
heat to medium–low and simmer for 5 minutes. Cool slightly, then
add the mint, parsley and lemon juice and puree using a hand
blender (or puree in batches in a blender) until smooth.

Season to taste with salt and pepper, then reheat over low heat.
Ladle the soup into serving bowls, drizzle over the yoghurt and oil
and sprinkle with the dukkah. Serve with the lemon wedges and
flatbread. **Serves 4–6**

* Dukkah is a spice, nut and seed blend from delis and Middle
Eastern food shops.

Squid with chilli lime salt and homemade chilli jam

4 squid tubes, with tentacles
Sunflower oil, to deep-fry
2 eggwhites
½ cup (100g) rice flour

Chilli jam
2 tomatoes, chopped
1 cup (220g) caster sugar
4 long red chillies,
   roughly chopped
¼ cup (60ml) white vinegar
2 tbs lime juice
1 garlic clove, finely chopped
1 tbs fish sauce

Chilli lime salt
2 tsp dried chilli flakes
2 tbs caster sugar
⅓ cup (20g) fried Asian
   shallots*
Finely grated zest of 1 lime
2 tbs sea salt

Begin the chilli jam a day ahead.

For the chilli jam, place the tomato and sugar in a bowl, cover and stand at room temperature overnight. The next day, place the tomato mixture and chilli in a food processor and pulse to combine. Transfer to a saucepan over low heat and add the vinegar, lime juice, garlic and fish sauce, stirring to dissolve the sugar. Increase the heat to medium and simmer, stirring occasionally, for 15–20 minutes until thick and jammy. Set aside to cool.

For the salt, place all the ingredients in a mini food processor or mortar and pestle and crush to a powder. Set aside.

Separate the squid tubes from the tentacles. Clean the squid tubes, then remove and discard the beaks from the tentacles. Slice the squid tubes lengthways to open up, then lightly score the inside. Cut into 2cm-wide strips. Set aside.

Half-fill a deep-fryer or large saucepan with the oil and heat to 190°C (a cube of bread will turn golden in 30 seconds).

Lightly whisk the eggwhites in a bowl until frothy. Place the flour in a separate shallow bowl and season. Dip the squid tubes and tentacles first in the eggwhite, then in the flour, shaking off any excess. In batches, deep-fry the squid for 1 minute or until crispy – be careful not to overcook or the squid will become tough. Remove with a slotted spoon and drain on paper towel.

Sprinkle the fried squid pieces with the chilli lime salt and serve with the chilli jam. **Serves 4–6**

* Fried Asian shallots are available from Asian food shops and selected supermarkets.

Spicy chicken salad in wonton cups

Olive oil spray

24 wonton wrappers*

¾ cup (185ml) orange juice

¼ cup (60ml) Chinese black vinegar*

2 tbs soy sauce

2 tbs sesame oil

1 tbs honey

1 tbs mirin (Japanese rice wine)*

1 tbs finely grated ginger

1 garlic clove, finely chopped

1 long red chilli, seeds removed, finely chopped

½ barbecued chicken, meat shredded

1 cup (80g) finely shredded wombok (Chinese cabbage)*

1 small carrot, cut into matchsticks

½ cup coriander leaves, finely chopped

½ cup mint leaves, finely chopped, plus extra to garnish

¼ cup roasted peanuts, chopped

Preheat the oven to 180°C. Spray a 6-hole Texas (185ml) muffin pan with oil.

On a work surface, lay out 4 wonton wrappers in a square with the edges slightly overlapping. Brush the overlapping sides with water so the wrappers stick together to form a large square. Repeat with the remaining wonton wrappers. Use these large squares to line the muffin holes – you will have to fold some of the edges down to form a cup shape. Spray with more oil and place in the oven for 7 minutes or until crisp and golden, watching carefully as they brown easily.

Meanwhile, place the orange juice in a small saucepan over medium-high heat. Bring to the boil, then simmer for 3 minutes or until reduced by half. Allow to cool, then combine with the vinegar, soy sauce, sesame oil, honey, mirin, ginger, garlic and chilli.

Toss the chicken, wombok, carrot, coriander, mint and peanuts with the dressing. Pile into the wonton cups, garnish with the mint leaves and serve immediately. **Makes 6**

* Available from Asian food shops and selected supermarkets.

Crab, coconut and green mango salad

1 green mango*, peeled

1 cup mint leaves

1 cup coriander leaves

2 kaffir lime leaves*, inner
   stem removed, very finely
   shredded

1½ tsp pickled ginger, thinly
   sliced

250g fresh crabmeat*

¼ cup (15g) shredded
   coconut, toasted

⅓ cup (50g) chopped roasted
   peanuts

Dressing

2 garlic cloves

1 small red chilli, seeds
   removed, finely chopped

1½ tbs fish sauce

2 tbs lime juice

1 tbs grated palm sugar* or
   brown sugar

2 tbs extra virgin olive oil

For the dressing, place the garlic and chilli in a mortar and pestle, then pound to a coarse paste. Add fish sauce, lime juice and sugar and stir to dissolve the sugar. Whisk in the olive oil and set aside.

Finely shred the mango (a mandoline is ideal), then place in a bowl with the mint, coriander, kaffir lime, ginger, crabmeat, coconut and peanuts.

To serve, drizzle the dressing over the salad and toss to combine.

Serves 4

* Green mango, kaffir lime leaves and palm sugar are available from Asian food shops. Crabmeat is available from fishmongers.

Hot-smoked salmon salad with Thai flavours

8 quail eggs*

2 green mangoes* or 1 green
   papaya*, shredded (a
   mandoline is ideal)

3 small red chillies, seeds
   removed, finely chopped

1 Asian red eschalot*, thinly
   sliced

1 cup each coriander, mint
   and Thai basil* leaves

2 x 175g hot-smoked salmon*
   portions

50g salmon roe*

2 tbs fried Asian shallots*

2 tbs peanuts, roughly
   chopped

Dressing

3 large red chillies, seeds
   removed, finely chopped

2 small red chillies, seeds
   removed, finely chopped

2 garlic cloves, finely
   chopped

50g grated palm sugar*
   or brown sugar

50ml fish sauce

100ml lime juice

For the dressing, shake all the ingredients in a sealed jar until well combined. Taste and adjust balance of sweet, sour and salty if necessary.

Place the quail eggs in a small saucepan of cold water, bring to the boil, then cook for 3 minutes to soft-boil. Drain, refresh in cold water, then peel and halve. Set aside until needed.

Combine the mango or papaya, chilli, eschalot, coriander, mint and Thai basil in a bowl. Flake the salmon into rough pieces, discarding any skin and bones, then toss with the salad and enough dressing to moisten.

Divide the salad among serving bowls. Top with the quail eggs and a spoonful of salmon roe. Garnish with the fried Asian shallots and peanuts. **Serves 4**

* Quail eggs, green mango, green papaya, Thai basil, fried shallots and palm sugar are from Asian food shops. Hot-smoked salmon is from supermarkets and gourmet food shops. Salmon roe is from delis and fishmongers.

Coronation prawns with Bombay mix

2 tbs sunflower oil

1 large onion, finely chopped

3 tbs (¼ cup) tikka curry
    paste*

2 tbs mango chutney, plus
    extra to serve

1 cup (300g) mayonnaise

150g thick Greek-style
    yoghurt

500g peeled, cooked prawns
    (tails intact)

3 spring onions, thinly sliced

3 celery stalks, thinly sliced
    on an angle, plus celery
    leaves to garnish

1 mango, thinly sliced

Coriander leaves and Bombay
    mix (Bhuja)*, to serve

Heat the oil in a frypan over medium heat. Add the onion and cook, stirring, for 2–3 minutes until softened, then add the curry paste and stir for 1 minute or until fragrant. Stir in the mango chutney and ⅓ cup (80ml) water, then remove from the heat and allow to cool.

Place the curry mixture in a food processor or blender with the mayonnaise and two-thirds (100g) of the yoghurt and process until smooth.

Place the prawns, spring onion, celery and mango in a bowl. Add the curry dressing and gently toss to combine. Place on a serving platter, drizzle with the remaining yoghurt, then scatter with the Bombay mix, celery leaves and coriander leaves. Serve with extra mango chutney and Bombay mix, if desired. **Serves 4**

* Tikka curry paste and Bombay mix are available from selected supermarkets and Indian food shops.

Crispy fish burritos with salsa criolla

1⅔ cups (250g)
   self-raising flour
Pinch of dried chilli flakes
1 egg, lightly beaten
375ml chilled lager
Sunflower oil, to deep-fry
4 x 180g flathead fillets,
   halved lengthways
8 flour tortillas
Sour cream, thinly sliced
   avocado and lime wedges,
   to serve

Salsa criolla
2 vine-ripened tomatoes,
   seeds removed, finely
   chopped
1 small red onion, finely
   chopped
1 garlic clove, crushed
1 long red chilli, seeds
   removed, finely chopped
¼ cup (60ml) red wine
   vinegar
1 tbs caster sugar
¼ cup chopped coriander
   leaves, plus extra to serve
2 tbs olive oil

Place the flour, chilli flakes and 1 teaspoon sea salt in a bowl. Add the egg, then gradually whisk in the lager until just combined. Cover and chill for 30 minutes.

Meanwhile, for the salsa criolla, place all the ingredients in a bowl, season, then stir well to combine. Set aside.

Preheat the oven to 150°C.

Half-fill a large saucepan or deep-fryer with the oil and heat to 190°C (if you don't have a kitchen thermometer, a cube of bread dropped into the oil will turn golden after 30 seconds when the oil is hot enough). Pat the fish dry with paper towel, then season. In batches, dip the fish into the beer batter, shaking off excess, then deep-fry for 3–4 minutes until crisp and golden. Remove with a slotted spoon and drain on paper towel. Transfer to a baking tray and keep warm in the oven while you cook the remaining fish.

Enclose the tortillas in foil and warm in the oven as you cook the final batch of fish.

Spread the tortillas with a little sour cream, then top with the avocado, fish, some salsa criolla and coriander sprigs. Season, then roll up and serve with the lime wedges and remaining salsa.

Serves 4

Spicy prawns with harissa couscous

2 small red chillies, seeds
  removed, chopped
Juice of ½ lemon
3 garlic cloves
1 tbs smoked paprika
  (pimenton)
⅓ cup (80ml) olive oil
1 tbs red wine vinegar
16 large green prawns

Harissa couscous
1 cup (200g) couscous
1 tsp harissa*
1 tbs pomegranate
  molasses*
2 tsp baharat spice mix*
Juice of ½ lemon
1 red onion, thinly sliced
Seeds of 1 pomegranate
2 cups coriander leaves

Place the chilli, lemon juice, garlic, paprika, oil and vinegar in a mini food processor and whiz until you have a smooth paste.

Coat the prawns in the marinade, cover and chill for 1 hour.

For the harissa couscous, place the couscous in a bowl and pour over 400ml boiling water. Stir to combine, then add the harissa, pomegranate molasses, baharat and lemon juice. Season with salt, then cover and set aside for 10 minutes or until the water is absorbed. Fluff the couscous with a fork and stir through the onion, pomegranate seeds and coriander leaves. Set aside.

Meanwhile, preheat a chargrill pan or barbecue to medium-high heat. Cook the prawns for 2 minutes each side or until just cooked through. Serve the prawns with the harissa couscous. **Serves 4**

* Harissa (a North African chilli paste), pomegranate molasses and baharat spice mix are available from Middle Eastern food shops and selected delis.

Moroccan-style fish with preserved lemons and olives

¼ cup (60ml) vegetable oil

1 onion, thinly sliced

2 tbs chermoula*

4 tomatoes, seeds removed, cut into wedges

600ml fish stock

¼ preserved lemon*, flesh and white pith discarded, skin thinly sliced

8 small chat potatoes, cut into wedges

4 x 150g firm white fish cutlets or fillets (such as jewfish)

16 niçoise or other small black olives

1 tbs chopped coriander leaves

2 tbs chopped mint leaves, plus extra leaves to garnish

Couscous, to serve

Heat half the oil in a frypan over medium heat. Add the onion and cook, stirring occasionally, for 3–4 minutes until softened. Add the chermoula, tomato, stock and half the preserved lemon, then bring to the boil. Reduce the heat to low and simmer for 20 minutes until slightly thickened. Add the potato and simmer for 6 minutes until tender.

Meanwhile, heat the remaining oil in a frypan over medium-high heat. Season the fillets with salt and pepper, then cook for 2–3 minutes each side until almost cooked through.

Add the fish to the sauce with the remaining preserved lemon, the olives, coriander and mint. Warm through, then garnish with the extra mint and serve with the couscous. **Serves 4**

* Preserved lemon and chermoula (a North African herb and spice paste) are available from delis and gourmet shops.

Peppered tuna with green tea noodles

4 x 180g tuna steaks
⅓ cup (80ml) sunflower oil
2 tbs sansho pepper* or
  Sichuan pepper*
200g green tea soba
  noodles*
1 cup frozen, podded
  edamame (soy beans)*
2 tbs mirin (Japanese
  rice wine)*
2 tbs soy sauce
1 tbs rice vinegar
1 tsp sesame oil
Seaweed salad (wakame)*,
  to serve

Brush the tuna steaks with 1 tablespoon sunflower oil. Mix the sansho or Sichuan pepper, 2 tablespoons freshly ground black pepper and 1 teaspoon sea salt in a bowl, then rub onto the tuna. Set aside while you cook the noodles.

Cook the noodles in boiling, salted water according to the packet instructions, adding the edamame for the final 3 minutes of cooking time. Drain and refresh under cold water. Set aside.

Place 1 tablespoon sunflower oil on the flat plate of a barbecue or in a frypan over medium-high heat. Cook the tuna for 1 minute each side for rare.

Place the mirin, soy sauce, rice vinegar, sesame oil and the remaining sunflower oil in a bowl, stir to combine, then toss with the noodles and edamame. Divide the noodles among serving plates and top with the tuna. Serve with the seaweed salad.
Serves 4

* Available from Asian food shops.

Spicy squid spaghetti

1 tbs extra virgin olive oil

3 garlic cloves, finely
   chopped

⅓ cup (80ml) dry red wine

400g can chopped tomatoes

2 tsp harissa* (or to taste)

500g baby squid, cleaned,
   tubes lightly scored

400g spaghetti (or other long
   thin pasta)

2 tbs chopped flat-leaf
   parsley leaves

Heat the oil in a frypan over medium heat. Add the garlic and cook, stirring, for 1–2 minutes until softened. Add the wine, tomato and harissa and cook, stirring occasionally, for 1–2 minutes. Add the squid and season to taste. Reduce the heat to low and simmer for 30–40 minutes until the squid is tender, adding a little water if the sauce becomes too thick.

Meanwhile, cook the spaghetti in a large saucepan of boiling, salted water according to the packet instructions. Drain the pasta and divide among serving bowls, then top with the squid mixture and garnish with the parsley. **Serves 4**

* Harissa (a North African chilli paste) is from delis and Middle Eastern food shops.

Chorizo-crusted blue-eye with spiced beans

4 x 180g skinless blue-eye
fillets
1 tbs olive oil
1 onion, finely chopped
1 tsp ground cumin
½ tsp ground turmeric
1 tsp smoked paprika
(pimenton)
1 tbs tomato paste
400g can chopped tomatoes
¼ cup (55g) caster sugar
100ml red wine vinegar
2 x 400g cans cannellini
beans, rinsed, drained
Salad leaves and lemon
wedges, to serve

Chorizo crust
1 dried chorizo sausage,
casing removed, chopped
1¼ cups (105g) fresh
sourdough breadcrumbs
20g unsalted butter
1 garlic clove, chopped
2 tbs chopped flat-leaf
parsley leaves
½ tsp smoked paprika
(pimenton)

Preheat the oven to 200°C and line a baking tray with baking paper.

For the chorizo crust, place all the ingredients in a food processor and whiz until well combined.

Season the fish, then pat the chorizo mixture on top. Place on the baking tray and chill for 10 minutes.

Meanwhile, place the oil in a frypan over low heat. Add the onion and cook, stirring, for 2–3 minutes until softened. Add the cumin, turmeric and paprika, then cook, stirring, for 1 minute or until fragrant. Add the tomato paste and cook, stirring, for a further 1 minute, then add the chopped tomatoes, sugar and vinegar, stirring to dissolve the sugar. Cook for 5 minutes or until reduced by one-third. Add the beans and cook for a further 5 minutes or until slightly thickened – add a little water if the mixture is too thick. Season and keep warm.

Bake the fish for 8–10 minutes until the crust is golden and the fish is just cooked. Serve with the spiced beans, salad leaves and lemon wedges. **Serves 4**

My fish curry

2 tbs sunflower oil

1 tsp yellow mustard seeds

1 onion, sliced

1 cinnamon quill

3cm piece ginger, grated

4 garlic cloves, thinly sliced

1 long red chilli, seeds
   removed, thinly sliced

1 tsp ground cumin

2 tsp ground coriander

½ tsp ground turmeric

½ tsp garam masala

12 fresh curry leaves*

2 tomatoes, seeds removed,
   cut into thin wedges

300ml fish or chicken stock

400ml coconut milk

450g boneless, skinless firm
   white fish fillets (such as
   blue-eye), cut into 3cm
   cubes

Coriander leaves, to garnish

Steamed basmati rice,
   pappadams and tomato
   kasundi or chutney, to
   serve

Heat the oil in a deep frypan over medium heat. Add the mustard seeds and cook for 1 minute or until they start to pop. Add the onion, cinnamon and 1 teaspoon salt and cook, stirring occasionally, for 2–3 minutes until the onion has softened. Add the ginger, garlic, chilli, dry spices, curry leaves, tomato and ½ cup (125ml) stock and cook for 3–4 minutes until nearly all the liquid has evaporated.

Add the coconut milk and remaining stock and simmer over medium heat for 5 minutes. Add the fish and simmer for a further 5 minutes or until the fish is cooked through. Season with salt and pepper. Garnish with the coriander and serve with the rice, pappadams and tomato kasundi or chutney. **Serves 4**

* Available from selected greengrocers and Asian food shops.

Teriyaki salmon with wasabi and avocado sauce

4 x 180g skinless salmon
  fillets
100ml soy sauce
100ml mirin (Japanese rice
  wine)*
Juice of 1 lemon
3 tsp wasabi paste*,
  or to taste
2 avocados, flesh chopped
1 tbs sunflower oil
Japanese pickled ginger*
  and lime wedges, to serve

Place the salmon fillets in a snap-lock bag. Combine the soy sauce and mirin in a bowl and place ¼ cup (60ml) of the mixture in the bag with the salmon, seal and marinate in the fridge for up to a day ahead.

Combine half the lemon juice with the remaining soy mixture. Place in dipping bowls.

Place the wasabi, avocado and remaining lemon juice in a food processor. Process until smooth and season to taste.

Heat a large non-stick frypan over medium heat. Remove the salmon from the bag, reserving any remaining marinade, then rub with the oil. Cook for 2–3 minutes each side until cooked but still a little rare in the centre. Add the reserved marinade and allow to bubble for 1 minute.

Serve with the wasabi and avocado sauce, soy dipping sauce, pickled ginger and lime wedges. **Serves 4**

* Available from selected supermarkets and Asian food shops.

Chargrilled swordfish with chermoula and potato smash

1kg waxy potatoes (such as
  kipfler)
4 x 180g swordfish steaks
100g rocket, roughly
  chopped
Micro herbs* or coriander
  leaves, to serve

Chermoula
1 bunch coriander, chopped
2 small red chillies, seeds
  removed, finely chopped
4 garlic cloves, chopped
1 tsp ground cumin
1 tsp sweet paprika
1 tsp ground coriander
½ cup (125ml) extra virgin
  olive oil
Finely grated zest and juice
  of 2 lemons

For the chermoula, place all the ingredients in a blender. Season, then whiz to combine. Set aside.

Place the potatoes in a saucepan of cold, salted water. Bring to the boil over medium heat and cook for 15–20 minutes until tender. Drain, then return the potatoes to the pan and roughly crush with a fork. Stir in two-thirds of the chermoula and keep warm.

Meanwhile, heat a chargrill pan or non-stick frypan over medium-high heat. Coat the swordfish in the remaining chermoula and cook for 2 minutes each side or until just cooked through.

To serve, fold the rocket into the potato smash and divide among serving plates. Place the swordfish on top and garnish with the herbs. **Serves 4**

* Micro herbs are available from selected greengrocers and growers' markets.

Prawn pilau

1 cup (200g) basmati rice

1 tsp ground turmeric

¼ cup (60ml) sunflower oil

1 onion, finely chopped

1 cinnamon quill

5 cloves

6 cardamom pods, bruised

10 fresh curry leaves*

1 lemongrass stem (inner core only), finely chopped

4 garlic cloves, finely chopped

5cm piece ginger, finely grated

600g peeled green prawns

30g unsalted butter

1 tbs chopped coriander leaves

1 tbs chopped dill

Lemon wedges and mango chutney, to serve

Place the rice and ½ teaspoon turmeric in a saucepan of cold, salted water. Bring to a simmer over medium heat. Cook for 5 minutes, then drain and set aside.

Meanwhile, place the oil in a deep frypan (with a lid) over medium-low heat. Add the onion, cinnamon, cloves, cardamom, curry leaves and lemongrass, then cook, stirring, for 5–6 minutes until the onion has softened. Stir in the garlic, ginger and remaining ½ teaspoon turmeric, then add the prawns and cook, stirring, for 2–3 minutes until just cooked. Add the rice, stirring to coat the grains, then add ½ cup (125ml) water and 1 teaspoon salt. Cover with a lid and cook for 5 minutes. Remove from the heat and stand, covered, for 5 minutes or until all the liquid has been absorbed – don't be tempted to lift the lid early as you will lose the steam that cooks the rice.

Add the butter to the pilau and fluff up with a fork. Stir in the herbs and serve with the lemon wedges and mango chutney.
Serves 4

*·From greengrocers and selected supermarkets.

Tandoori swordfish with lemon achar

3 tbs (75g) tandoori paste
3 tbs (70g) thick Greek-style
   yoghurt
4 x 180g swordfish steaks
1 tbs vegetable oil
2 tsp black mustard seeds
3 preserved lemon quarters*,
   white pith and flesh
   removed, rind thinly sliced
1 long red chilli, seeds
   removed, thinly sliced
1 tsp ground turmeric
12 fresh curry leaves*
1 tbs white wine vinegar
2 tsp caster sugar
2 tomatoes, seeds removed,
   sliced
Pappadams and steamed
   basmati rice, to serve

Combine the tandoori paste and yoghurt in a shallow dish. Add the swordfish steaks and turn to coat in the mixture, then cover and marinate in the fridge for 1 hour.

Meanwhile, for the lemon achar, heat the oil in a frypan over medium heat. Add the mustard seeds and cook for 1 minute or until they start to pop. Add the preserved lemon, chilli, turmeric and curry leaves and cook, stirring, for 3 minutes. Combine the vinegar and sugar in a small bowl, stirring to dissolve the sugar, then add to the pan with the tomato. Stir to combine, then remove from the heat and set aside to cool.

Preheat a chargrill pan or barbecue on medium-high, then cook the fish for 2 minutes each side or until cooked but still moist in the centre. Serve the swordfish with the achar, pappadams and rice.
Serves 4

* Preserved lemons are from gourmet shops and delis. Fresh curry leaves are from selected greengrocers and Asian shops.

Blackened salmon with papaya mojo

1 tbs dried oregano

1 tbs sweet paprika

3 garlic cloves, crushed

¼ cup (60ml) extra virgin
  olive oil

1kg piece skinless salmon
  fillet, pin-boned

2 tbs sunflower oil

Lime halves, to serve

Papaya mojo

¼ cup (60ml) extra virgin
  olive oil

1 small red onion, thinly
  sliced

1 papaya, cut into cubes

2 x 400g cans black turtle
  beans*, drained, rinsed

1 bunch coriander, leaves
  roughly chopped

Finely grated zest and juice
  of 2 limes

Preheat the oven to 180°C.

Place the oregano, paprika, garlic and olive oil in a bowl and season. Place the fish on a chopping board and rub the marinade into the topside of the fish.

Place the sunflower oil in a flameproof, non-stick roasting pan over high heat. Warm for 1–2 minutes until the oil is smoking, then add the fish, marinated-side down, and cook for 5–6 minutes until the flesh has blackened. Transfer to the oven, then roast for 10 minutes or until just cooked, but still a little rare in the centre.

Meanwhile, for the papaya mojo, place all the ingredients together in a bowl, season, then gently toss to combine. Set aside.

Invert the fish onto a platter and top with the papaya mojo. Serve with the lime halves. **Serves 6–8**

* Available from delis and gourmet food shops.

Jerk chicken

4 chicken drumsticks (skin on)
4 chicken thigh cutlets
   (skin on)
Lemon halves and mixed
   salad leaves, to serve

Jerk marinade
1 onion, chopped
2 small red chillies, seeds
   removed, chopped
2 garlic cloves, chopped
4cm piece ginger, chopped
2 tsp thyme leaves
¼ tsp ground allspice
½ cup (125ml) cider vinegar
½ cup (125ml) soy sauce
1 tbs honey
⅓ cup (80ml) olive oil

For the jerk marinade, place the onion, chilli, garlic, ginger and
thyme in a food processor and whiz until chopped. Add the
allspice, vinegar, soy sauce, honey and oil. Whiz until a thick paste
forms.

Score the flesh side of the chicken, then coat well in the
marinade. Cover and refrigerate for 3 hours or overnight.

Preheat the oven to 180°C. Place a wire rack over a roasting pan
filled with 2cm water.

Drain the chicken, reserving the marinade, then place the chicken
on the rack. Bake for 30 minutes, then brush with the reserved
marinade. Bake the chicken for a further 30 minutes or until cooked
through.

Serve the jerk chicken hot or cold with the lemon halves and
mixed salad leaves. **Serves 4–6**

Bombay sliders

500g chicken mince

¼ cup chopped coriander
leaves, plus extra leaves
to serve

¼ cup finely chopped
spring onion

1 tsp ground cumin

1 small red chilli, seeds
removed, chopped

2cm piece ginger, grated

¾ cup (225g) whole-egg
mayonnaise

2 tbs mild curry powder

1 tbs tomato sauce (ketchup)

1 tbs thick Greek-style
yoghurt

1 garlic clove, crushed

2 tbs olive oil

12 small brioche or mini
burger buns*, split, toasted

Mango chutney and micro
salad leaves* (optional),
to serve

Place the chicken mince, coriander, spring onion, cumin, chilli, ginger, ¼ cup (75g) mayonnaise and 1½ tablespoons curry powder in a bowl. Mix well to combine, season, then shape into 12 small patties. Chill for 30 minutes to firm up.

Place the tomato sauce, yoghurt, garlic, and remaining ½ cup (150g) mayonnaise and 2 teaspoons curry powder in a bowl. Season, then stir to combine. Set aside.

Place the oil in a frypan over medium-high heat. In batches, cook the patties for 2–3 minutes each side or until cooked through.

To serve, spread the base of each bun with some mango chutney, then top with the chicken patties, curry mayonnaise, extra coriander and micro salad leaves, if desired. Sandwich with the bun tops and secure with toothpicks or small skewers. **Makes 12**

* Order mini burger buns from bakeries. Micro salad leaves are from selected greengrocers and growers' markets.

Angel hair pasta with larb

¼ cup (60ml) sunflower oil
150g mixed Asian
   mushrooms* (such as
   shiitake, shimeji and enoki),
   whole or sliced
1 tbs sesame oil
2 long red chillies, seeds
   removed, finely chopped
3cm piece ginger, grated
4 kaffir lime leaves*,
   inner stem removed,
   very finely shredded
500g chicken mince
2 tbs fish sauce
2 tbs light soy sauce
1 cup coriander leaves
2 cups Thai basil leaves*
Juice of 1 lime, plus lime
   halves to serve
500g angel hair pasta

Heat 2 tablespoons sunflower oil in a wok over high heat. Add the mushrooms and stir-fry for 1–2 minutes until starting to wilt. Remove from the wok and set aside.

Add 2 teaspoons sesame oil and the remaining sunflower oil to the wok, then add the chilli, ginger and kaffir lime leaves, and stir-fry for 30 seconds or until fragrant. Add the chicken and stir-fry for a further 3–4 minutes until browned all over. Return the mushrooms to the wok with the fish sauce, soy sauce, coriander and 1 cup Thai basil, then reduce the heat to low and cook until warmed through. Stir through the lime juice. Keep warm and set aside.

Meanwhile, cook the pasta according to the packet instructions. Drain, reserving ⅓ cup (80ml) cooking water. Return the pasta to the pan and toss with the reserved water and remaining sesame oil.

Divide the pasta among serving bowls, top with the larb, then garnish with the remaining Thai basil and serve with the lime halves.
Serves 4

* Asian mushrooms, kaffir lime leaves and Thai basil are available from Asian food shops and selected greengrocers.

Duck wonton soup

150g dried shiitake
   mushrooms*
½ Chinese roast duck*
½ bunch coriander,
   leaves picked, stems
   and roots reserved
3cm piece ginger, peeled
2 tbs light soy sauce
8 spring onions, trimmed
2 tbs oyster sauce
32 wonton wrappers*
2 baby bok choy, halved
1 long red chilli, thinly sliced

Soak the shiitake mushrooms in 1 cup (250ml) boiling water
for 15 minutes. Drain the mushrooms, then finely chop the caps,
reserving the stalks, and set aside.

Finely chop the duck meat, reserving the bones, and set aside.
Roughly chop the coriander stems and roots, then set aside.

Place the mushroom stalks, duck bones, coriander stems and
roots, ginger, soy sauce and 4 spring onions in a saucepan with
1.5 litres (6 cups) cold water and bring to the boil. Reduce the heat
to low and simmer for 1 hour, skimming the surface occasionally.
Strain through a sieve into a clean saucepan, discarding the solids.

Meanwhile, finely chop the remaining spring onions and most
of the coriander leaves and place in a bowl with the duck meat,
chopped mushrooms and oyster sauce, then mix to combine.
Arrange the wonton wrappers on a clean work surface and place
1 teaspoon duck mixture in the centre of each. Brush the edges
with cold water and lift the corners up to meet in the centre, then
pinch to seal. Cover the wontons with a damp tea towel and chill
until ready to serve.

Return the stock to medium-high heat. Add the bok choy and
cook for 2–3 minutes until tender. Keep warm.

In batches, cook the wontons in boiling salted water for
1–2 minutes until they float to the surface. Remove with a slotted
spoon and add to the soup. Ladle the soup into serving bowls,
garnish with the chilli and remaining coriander leaves and serve.
Serves 4–6

* Dried shiitake mushrooms and wonton wrappers are available
from Asian food shops. Chinese roast duck is from Chinese
takeaway shops.

Chilli rice with Chinese barbecued duck

1 cup (200g) jasmine rice
(or use 3 cups leftover
cooked rice)
1 tbs sunflower oil
1 large red onion, thinly
sliced
2 eggplants, cut into 2cm
cubes
4 tbs chilli jam*
200g baby spinach leaves
1 Chinese barbecued duck*,
meat removed, chopped
½ cup mint leaves
½ cup coriander leaves
Sliced long red chilli, to
garnish

Cook the rice according to packet instructions. Cool.
Meanwhile, heat the oil in a wok over medium-high heat.
Add the onion and stir-fry for 5 minutes or until starting to brown.
Add the eggplant and cook, stirring, for 2–3 minutes until the
eggplant starts to soften and turn golden.
Add the rice to the eggplant with the chilli jam, spinach leaves
and duck meat and cook, stirring, for a further minute or until
heated through. Remove from the heat, stir through the mint and
coriander, then serve garnished with the chilli. **Serves 4**

* Chilli jam is available from selected supermarkets and delis, or
you could make your own using the recipe on page 28. Duck is from
Asian barbecue shops.

Salt and pepper quail with chilli sauce

⅓ cup (50g) cornflour
2½ tbs ground Sichuan
  peppercorns*
1 tbs dried chilli flakes
6 quail legs* and 6 quail
  breasts*
Sunflower oil, to deep-fry
Sweet chilli sauce and lime
  wedges, to serve

Seasoned salt
1 tsp sea salt
1 tsp ground Sichuan
  peppercorns*
1 tsp dried chilli flakes

Preheat the oven to 170°C. Line a baking tray with baking paper.

Combine the cornflour, Sichaun peppercorns and chilli flakes in a bowl with 1 tablespoon black pepper. Pat the quail pieces dry with paper towel, then toss in the flour mixture to coat, shaking off any excess. Set aside.

For the seasoned salt, combine all the ingredients in a bowl and set aside.

Half-fill a deep-fryer or large saucepan with the oil and heat to 190°C (a cube of bread will turn golden in 30 seconds).

In batches, deep-fry the quail for 2–3 minutes until golden and crisp. Remove with a slotted spoon and drain on paper towel. Transfer the quail to the lined tray and bake for 5 minutes until cooked through.

Sprinkle the seasoned salt over the quail, then serve with the sweet chilli sauce and lime wedges. **Serves 4**

* Ground Sichuan peppercorns are from Asian food shops and Herbie's Spices (herbies.com.au). Quail legs and breasts are from poultry shops and Game Farm (gamefarm.com.au).

Chicken and eggplant laksa

4 slices chargrilled eggplant*,
   drained, cut into strips
250g thick rice-stick noodles
3–4 tbs laksa paste
400ml can coconut milk
600ml chicken stock
4 small chicken breast fillets,
   thinly sliced
1 lemongrass stem (pale part
   only), bruised
2 kaffir lime leaves*
150g sugar snap peas, halved
   lengthways or shredded
1 tsp brown sugar
Zest and juice of 1 lime
Thai basil* and coriander
   leaves, to serve

Pat the eggplant with paper towel to remove excess oil.

Soak the noodles in boiling water according to packet instructions until soft. Drain, then rinse in cold water and set aside.

Heat a wok over medium heat and stir-fry the laksa paste for 1 minute or until fragrant. Stir in the coconut milk and stock, then bring to a simmer. Add the chicken, lemongrass and kaffir lime leaves and simmer for 6–8 minutes or until the chicken is cooked through. Add the peas and eggplant and simmer for 2 minutes or until the peas are just cooked. Stir in the sugar, lime zest and juice.

Divide the noodles among serving bowls and top with the laksa. Garnish with the Thai basil and coriander, then serve. **Serves 4**

* Chargrilled eggplant is from delis and supermarkets. Kaffir lime leaves and Thai basil are from greengrocers and Asian food shops.

Chicken tikka with minted yoghurt

5 cardamom pods

1 tbs sunflower oil

1 garlic clove, finely chopped

2cm piece ginger, grated

1 tsp ground turmeric

1 tsp ground cumin

1 tsp ground fenugreek

2 tbs lemon juice

1/3 cup (95g) thick Greek-style
   yoghurt

4 chicken thigh fillets,
   trimmed, quartered

1 tbs finely chopped mint
   leaves, plus extra to serve

4 pieces mountain bread
   or lavash bread

Butter lettuce leaves, to serve

Lightly crush the cardamom pods to remove the seeds, discarding
the green husk.

Heat the oil in a frypan over low heat. Add the garlic, ginger,
turmeric, cumin, fenugreek and cardamom seeds and cook, stirring,
for 1 minute until fragrant. Cool slightly, then transfer to a ceramic
or glass dish. Stir in the lemon juice and 2 tablespoons yoghurt,
then season well with salt and pepper. Add the chicken and turn to
coat in the mixture. Cover and marinate in the fridge for at least
4 hours, or overnight.

Heat a lightly oiled chargrill pan or barbecue on medium-high
heat. In batches if necessary, cook the chicken for 4 minutes on
each side or until cooked through.

Meanwhile, stir the chopped mint into the remaining yoghurt,
then season to taste with salt and pepper.

Serve the chicken hot or cold, with the flatbread, minted yoghurt,
lettuce and extra mint leaves. **Serves 4**

Chicken with chilli chocolate

1 tbs olive oil

20g unsalted butter

4 chicken breast fillets

100g pancetta, cut into strips

2 celery stalks, chopped

1 onion, sliced

2 garlic cloves, finely
chopped

150ml dry red wine

400ml chicken stock

400g can chopped tomatoes

50g chilli chocolate, broken
into small pieces

300g can red kidney beans,
rinsed, drained

Steamed rice, sliced red chilli,
coriander leaves (optional),
corn chips and avocado
wedges, to serve

Preheat the oven to 180°C.

Heat the oil and butter in a flameproof casserole over medium heat. Add the chicken and cook for 2–3 minutes each side until golden, then remove and set aside. Add the pancetta, celery and onion and cook, stirring, for 5 minutes until the vegetables soften. Add the garlic and wine and simmer for 2–3 minutes. Stir in the stock, tomatoes and chocolate, then return the chicken to the pan. Cover and transfer to the oven for 25 minutes or until the chicken is cooked through.

Remove the chicken from the pan, cover loosely with foil and set aside in a warm place. Return the pan to the stove over medium-high heat, add the beans and simmer for 4–5 minutes until thickened.

Slice the chicken and serve on the rice, with the sauce, chilli, and coriander if desired. Serve with the corn chips and avocado.

Serves 4

Chinese pork buns

2 tbs rice vinegar

2 tbs caster sugar

1 carrot, cut into matchsticks

2 Lebanese cucumbers, seeds removed, cut into matchsticks

¼ cup (60ml) sriracha chilli sauce*

¼ cup (60ml) mayonnaise (preferably Japanese*)

20 small (7cm) white bread rolls*, split

300g good-quality chicken liver pâté

600g Chinese roast pork belly*, sliced

1 cup coriander leaves

1 cup micro cress*

Combine the vinegar, sugar and 1 teaspoon salt in a bowl. Stir to dissolve the sugar. Add the carrot and cucumber and stand for at least 10 minutes. Drain well and set aside.

Combine the chilli sauce and mayonnaise in a bowl and set aside.

Lightly toast the buns, then spread the base of each with a generous amount of pâté. Fill the buns with slices of pork belly and top with a little pickled carrot and cucumber, coriander and micro cress. Drizzle with the chilli mayonnaise and serve. **Makes 20**

* Sriracha chilli sauce and Japanese mayonnaise are from Asian food shops. Small bread rolls are from selected bakeries. Chinese roast pork belly is from Chinese barbecue shops. Micro cress is from farmers' markets and selected greengrocers.

Sticky pork cutlets with spicy Asian slaw

4 x 170g pork cutlets

1 tbs sunflower oil

2 tbs soy sauce

1 tbs honey

Spicy Asian slaw

¼ white cabbage,
   finely shredded

¼ red cabbage,
   finely shredded

1 carrot, finely shredded

1 red onion, thinly sliced

1 cup mint leaves

1 cup coriander leaves

1 kaffir lime leaf*,
   finely shredded

¼ cup (60ml) rice vinegar

1 tbs caster sugar

2 tbs soy sauce

1½ tbs lime juice

2 tbs fish sauce

2 long red chillies, seeds
   removed, finely chopped

For the Asian slaw, place the cabbages, carrot, onion, mint, coriander and kaffir lime leaf in a bowl. Combine the rice vinegar, sugar, soy sauce, lime juice, fish sauce and chilli in a small bowl and whisk to combine. Toss the slaw with the dressing and set aside.

Drizzle the pork with the oil and season. Place a frypan over medium-high heat, then cook the pork for 2–3 minutes each side until golden. Reduce the heat to medium–low, then whisk the soy sauce and honey together and drizzle over the pork. Cook, turning, for a further 3–4 minutes until the pork chops are caramelised and cooked through. Serve with the spicy Asian slaw. **Serves 4**

* From greengrocers and Asian food shops.

Chorizo carbonara

4 good-quality fresh chorizo
　　or other spicy sausages
2 tbs olive oil
4 egg yolks
300ml pure (thin) cream
⅓ cup (25g) grated
　　parmesan, plus extra to
　　serve
400g spaghetti or fettuccine
2 tbs chopped flat-leaf
　　parsley leaves

Remove the casings from the chorizo and roll the meat into bite-sized balls (you should get about 40).

Heat the oil in a frypan over medium heat. In 2–3 batches, cook the meatballs, turning, for 2–3 minutes until browned and cooked through. Drain on paper towel.

Beat the egg yolks, cream and parmesan together in a bowl. Season well with salt and pepper, then set aside.

Meanwhile, cook the pasta in boiling, salted water according to the packet instructions. Drain the pasta, then return to the hot pan. Add the chorizo and the cream mixture and toss well to coat (the residual heat will gently cook the egg). Add the parsley and toss to combine, then serve with extra parmesan. **Serves 4**

Pork belly with caramel dressing

1kg boneless pork belly
  (skin on)
½ firmly packed cup (110g)
  brown sugar
⅓ cup (80ml) red wine
  vinegar
2 star anise
1 cup (250ml) chicken stock
Juice of 1 lime, plus wedges
  to serve
1 cup mint leaves
1 cup coriander leaves
1 cup Thai basil leaves*
3 spring onions, thinly sliced
1 long red chilli, seeds
  removed, thinly sliced

Preheat the oven to 220°C.

Score the pork belly skin at 1cm intervals. Place the pork on a rack in a roasting pan, skin-side up. Rub 2 tablespoons salt into the skin, then pour in enough water to fill the pan to just under the rack. Roast for 30 minutes or until the skin is crispy, then reduce the oven to 180°C and roast for a further 1½ hours or until the meat is tender, topping up with water as necessary.

Meanwhile, place the brown sugar, vinegar and star anise in a pan over low heat, stirring to dissolve the sugar. Simmer for 5 minutes, then add the chicken stock and simmer for 5–6 minutes until reduced by half. Add the lime juice and continue to reduce for 3–4 minutes until syrupy.

Carve the pork into bite-sized cubes and arrange on a platter. Drizzle with the caramel dressing, then scatter with the herbs, spring onion and chilli. Serve with the lime wedges to squeeze over.
Serves 6

* From Asian food shops and selected greengrocers.

Stir-fried pork wraps

8 dried shiitake mushrooms*

1 tbs sesame oil

2 tbs peanut oil

300g pork mince

¼ cup (60ml) light soy sauce

2 tbs Chinese rice wine
  (shaoxing)* or dry sherry

2 tsp caster sugar

2 tbs grated ginger

1 small red onion, thinly
  sliced

¼ savoy cabbage, very thinly
  sliced

2 tbs plum sauce, plus extra
  to serve

1 tbs chopped mint leaves,
  plus extra leaves to serve

2 carrots, thinly sliced into
  matchsticks

1 Lebanese cucumber, thinly
  sliced into matchsticks

8 small flour tortillas, warmed
  according to packet
  instructions

Soak the dried mushrooms in ¼ cup (60ml) boiling water for
10 minutes, then slice. Reserve the soaking liquid.

Heat the oils in a wok over medium-high heat. Add the pork and
stir-fry, breaking up with a spoon, for 3–4 minutes until lightly
browned. Add the soy sauce, rice wine or sherry, sugar, ginger,
onion, cabbage, plum sauce, chopped mint and shiitakes and
stir-fry for a further 2–3 minutes until the cabbage wilts.

Serve the pork, carrot, cucumber, warm tortillas and extra mint
and plum sauce separately, for people to make their own wraps.

Serves 4

* From Asian food shops and selected supermarkets.

Chinese barbecued pork and snow pea salad

400g Chinese barbecued
   pork*, thinly sliced
100g snow peas, trimmed,
   blanched
2 cups pea shoots
150g snow pea sprouts, ends
   trimmed
3 spring onions, sliced on
   an angle
1 small red capsicum, cut into
   matchsticks
2 tbs toasted sesame seeds

Dressing
3 tsp rice vinegar
1 small red chilli, seeds
   removed, finely chopped
¼ cup (60ml) light soy sauce
2cm piece ginger, cut into
   matchsticks
½ tsp sesame oil
1 star anise
2 tsp fresh lime juice

For the dressing, place the vinegar, chilli, soy sauce, ginger, sesame oil, star anise and lime juice in a small saucepan over low heat. Cook, stirring, for 2 minutes until warmed through. Remove from the heat and discard the star anise. Set aside to cool.

Combine the pork, snow peas, pea shoots, snow pea sprouts, spring onion and capsicum in a bowl. Toss with the dressing and transfer to a serving platter. Scatter with the sesame seeds.

Serves 4

* From Asian barbecue shops and selected supermarkets.

Sticky honey, soy and ginger pork ribs

5cm piece ginger, grated

6 garlic cloves, finely
   chopped

½ cup (125ml) light soy sauce

½ cup (175g) honey

½ cup (125ml) Chinese rice
   wine (shaoxing)*

1 tbs sweet chilli sauce

1.4kg pork ribs, cut into
   individual ribs

Coriander, lime wedges and
   steamed rice, to serve

Combine the ginger, garlic, soy sauce, honey, rice wine and sweet chilli sauce in a large zip-lock bag. Add the ribs, close the bag and shake to coat the pork thoroughly. Marinate in the fridge for at least 1 hour or overnight.

Preheat the oven to 180°C.

Remove the ribs from the bag, reserving the marinade, and place on a rack over a roasting pan filled with 1cm water. Roast for 35–40 minutes until sticky and golden. Remove the pork from the rack and set aside, loosely covered with foil, while you make the glaze.

For the glaze, place the marinade in a small saucepan over medium-high heat with any juices from the roasting pan. Bring to the boil, then allow to bubble for 4–5 minutes until the mixture is sticky, watching carefully to ensure it doesn't burn. Brush over ribs.

Place the glazed ribs on a serving platter with the coriander and lime wedges, then serve with the steamed rice. **Serves 3–4**

* From Asian food shops; substitute dry sherry.

Thai beef curry with holy basil

2 tbs sunflower oil

8 Asian red eschalots*, thinly sliced

400g beef fillet, cut into very thin strips

2 tbs Thai red curry paste

400ml can coconut milk

½ cup (75g) roasted peanuts, crushed, plus extra to serve

2 tbs grated palm sugar* or brown sugar

3 kaffir lime leaves*, plus extra shredded kaffir lime leaves to serve

¼ cup (60ml) fish sauce

1 cup Thai basil leaves* or basil leaves, plus extra to serve

Juice of ½ lime

Sliced long red chilli, bean spouts and steamed rice, to serve

Heat 1 tablespoon oil in a wok over high heat. Stir-fry half the eschalot for 30 seconds or until softened. Remove from the wok and set aside.

Add the remaining 1 tablespoon oil to the wok. In 3 batches, stir-fry the beef for 1–2 minutes until browned. Remove from the wok and set aside.

Add the curry paste and 100ml coconut milk to the wok, reduce the heat to medium–high and cook, stirring, for 1–2 minutes until fragrant and the oil has separated from the milk. Add the remaining coconut milk and simmer for 5 minutes. Add the peanuts, sugar and kaffir lime leaves and simmer for 5 minutes, then return the beef and cooked eschalot to the wok with the fish sauce. Cook for a further 30 seconds, then remove the wok from the heat and stir through the basil and lime juice.

Garnish the curry with the chilli, bean sprouts, shredded kaffir lime leaves, remaining eschalot and extra peanuts and basil. Serve with the steamed rice. **Serves 4**

* Available from Asian food shops.

Crisp stir-fried beef with orange

2 large strips of pared orange
  rind
⅓ cup (80ml) rice vinegar
½ cup (110g) caster sugar
¼ cup (60ml) soy sauce
⅓ cup (80ml) beef stock or
  water
2 tsp Sichuan peppercorns*
1 tsp cornflour
400g rump steak, trimmed
2 tbs sunflower oil
2 carrots, cut into matchsticks
2cm piece ginger, cut into
  thin matchsticks
2 garlic cloves, thinly sliced
1 tsp dried chilli flakes
1 red capsicum, very thinly
  sliced
Steamed rice, to serve
6 spring onions, thinly sliced
  lengthways

Preheat the oven to 150°C.

Place the orange rind on a baking tray and bake in the oven for 30 minutes or until dry.

Combine the vinegar, sugar, soy sauce and stock in a small bowl, then set aside.

Meanwhile, heat a small frypan over medium heat and dry-fry the peppercorns for 30 seconds or until fragrant. Place in a mortar with the orange rind and crush to a powder. Combine the powder with the cornflour and ½ teaspoon salt. Slice the beef 1cm thick, then cut into 1cm strips. Toss to coat in the spice mixture. Set aside for 15 minutes.

Heat the sunflower oil in a wok over high heat. In 2–3 batches, stir-fry the beef for 30 seconds until crisp, making sure the oil is very hot again before cooking the next batch. Drain on paper towel. Reduce the heat to medium–high, add the carrot, ginger, garlic, chilli and capsicum and stir-fry for 2–3 minutes, adding a little more oil if necessary. Return the beef to the wok with the sauce mixture, then stir-fry for 2 minutes or until well combined and heated through. Serve with the steamed rice, garnished with the spring onion. **Serves 4–6**

* Sichuan peppercorns are available from Asian food shops.

Lamb and harissa pizza with tabouli and yoghurt

2 tbs extra virgin olive oil,
   plus extra to serve
1 onion, finely chopped
1 garlic clove, finely chopped
500g lamb mince
2 tsp ground cumin
½ tsp ground cinnamon
1 cup (250ml) beef stock
1 tbs harissa*
2 tbs chopped flat-leaf
   parsley leaves
2 tbs chopped mint leaves
2 plain pizza bases
1 cup (260g) hummus
Thick Greek-style yoghurt,
   to serve

Tabouli
2 tbs burghul (cracked
   wheat)*
½ bunch flat-leaf parsley,
   leaves finely chopped
1 bunch mint, leaves finely
   chopped, plus extra to
   serve
2 tomatoes, seeds removed,
   finely chopped
2 red onions, finely chopped
1 tbs lemon juice

Preheat the oven to 200°C.

For the tabouli, soak the burghul in boiling water for 15 minutes, then drain. Toss the burghul with the remaining tabouli ingredients and season. Set aside.

Meanwhile, place the olive oil in a frypan over medium heat. Add the onion and cook, stirring, for 2–3 minutes until softened. Add the garlic and lamb, then cook, breaking up any lumps with a wooden spoon, for 4–5 minutes until the lamb is browned. Add the cumin, cinnamon, stock and 2 teaspoons harissa, then cook, stirring, for 1–2 minutes until the liquid has evaporated. Stir in the parsley and mint, then season.

Place each pizza base on a baking tray or pizza stone. Combine the hummus and remaining 2 teaspoons harissa, then spread over the pizza bases. Scatter with the lamb mixture, then bake for 5 minutes or until the edges are starting to crisp.

Scatter the tabouli over the pizzas and top with dollops of the yoghurt. Drizzle with the extra olive oil, then serve garnished with the extra mint. **Serves 4**

* Harissa (a North African chilli paste) is from delis and gourmet food shops. Burghul is from health food shops and selected supermarkets.

Moroccan cottage pie

2 tbs olive oil

1 onion, finely chopped

2 garlic cloves, chopped

650g lamb mince

1 tsp ground cumin

1 tsp ground cinnamon

½ tsp ground ginger

½ tsp chilli powder

2 tsp ground turmeric

2 tbs tomato paste

150ml red wine

150ml beef stock

½ cup (80g) roughly chopped
  pitted green olives

⅓ cup chopped mint leaves,
  plus small leaves to garnish

1kg pontiac potatoes,
  peeled, chopped

40g unsalted butter, chopped

½ cup (120g) creme fraiche
  or sour cream

Heat the olive oil in a large saucepan over medium-low heat. Add the onion and garlic and cook, stirring, for 2–3 minutes until softened. Add the lamb mince and cook, stirring, for 5–6 minutes until the meat is browned.

Add the dry spices (reserving 1 teaspoon turmeric for the potato) and the tomato paste, then cook for a further minute. Add the wine and stock, bring to a simmer, then reduce the heat to low and cook for 15–18 minutes until the meat is cooked and the sauce has thickened. Stir in the olives and mint. Transfer the mixture to a serving dish and set aside.

Meanwhile, cook the potato and remaining turmeric in a saucepan of boiling, salted water for 10–12 minutes until tender. Drain well and pass through a potato ricer or mash well. Season with sea salt and freshly ground black pepper. Stir in the butter and creme fraiche or sour cream.

Spread the mashed potato over the mince, then serve garnished with the small mint leaves. **Serves 4–6**

Thai-style braised beef cheeks

6 beef cheeks*

⅓ cup (50g) plain flour, seasoned

2 tbs sunflower oil

3 onions, sliced

4cm piece galangal*, sliced

1 lemongrass stem (pale part only), sliced

4cm piece fresh ginger, sliced into thin matchsticks

½ cup (135g) grated palm sugar* or brown sugar

3 garlic cloves, sliced

3 kaffir lime leaves*

3 long red chillies, seeds removed, thinly sliced

⅓ cup tamarind puree*

2 cups (500ml) beef stock

½ cup (125ml) fish sauce

Steamed rice, to serve

Herb salad

2 cups mixed Asian herbs (such as coriander, Thai basil* and Vietnamese mint*)

6 spring onions, sliced into very thin strips

2 tbs olive oil

1 tbs lime juice

Coat the beef in the flour, shaking off excess. Heat the oil in a large frypan over medium-high heat. In 2 batches, brown the beef for 1–2 minutes each side. Transfer to a slow-cooker or flameproof casserole. Add 1 litre (4 cups) water and all the remaining ingredients, reserving 1 sliced chilli for the salad. Stir to combine, then cover and cook on low heat for 7 hours (or overnight) in a slow-cooker, or in the oven at 170°C for 3 hours 30 minutes until the beef is very tender. Remove the beef and set aside. Reduce over medium-high heat until you have a thick sauce.

Just before serving, place the herb salad ingredients in a bowl with the reserved chilli, season with salt and toss to combine. Serve the beef on the rice, topped with the sauce and the herb salad.

Serves 6

* Order beef cheeks from your butcher. Substitute large pieces of chuck steak. All other ingredients are from Asian food shops.

My pho

200g flat rice-stick noodles

1 tbs sunflower oil

6 spring onions, sliced on an angle

2cm piece ginger, very thinly sliced

1 small red chilli, seeds removed, finely chopped

3 cups (750ml) beef consommé*

¼ cup (60ml) fish sauce

¼ cup (60ml) lime juice

100g bean sprouts, ends trimmed

¼ cup coriander leaves, plus extra to serve

¼ cup Thai basil leaves*, plus extra to serve

¼ cup mint leaves, plus extra to serve

400g thinly sliced rare roast beef

Soften the noodles in a bowl of boiling water according to packet instructions. Drain.

Meanwhile, heat the oil in a saucepan over medium heat. Add the spring onion, ginger and chilli and cook, stirring, for 2–3 minutes until the onion is soft. Add the consommé and 1 cup (250ml) water, then bring to the boil. Reduce the heat to low and simmer for 10 minutes. Stir in the fish sauce and lime juice.

Divide the noodles, bean sprouts and herbs among soup bowls, then ladle over the broth. Serve topped with the beef slices and extra herbs. **Serves 4**

* Beef consommé is available in cans and tetra packs from supermarkets. Thai basil is available from greengrocers and Asian food shops; substitute regular basil.

Lamb burgers with harissa mayonnaise and orange relish

1 tsp ground cumin

1 tsp ground coriander

1 tsp ground turmeric

1 tsp ground cinnamon

1 tbs honey

1kg lamb mince

½ red onion, finely chopped

3 garlic cloves, finely
   chopped

4 crusty bread rolls, split,
   toasted

Micro salad leaves*, to serve

Harissa mayonnaise

½ cup (150g) whole-egg
   mayonnaise

2 tbs harissa*

2 tbs finely chopped
   coriander

Orange relish

1 orange, peeled, pith
   removed, chopped

1 cup (120g) pitted
   kalamata olives, sliced

1 tbs slivered pistachios*

Combine the spices, honey, lamb, onion and garlic in a bowl and season. Divide the mixture into 4 portions, then use damp hands to form into burgers. Refrigerate for 30 minutes or until firm.

Meanwhile, for the harissa mayonnaise, combine the mayonnaise, harissa and coriander in a bowl and season. Cover and keep chilled until ready to serve.

For the orange relish, place the orange, olives and pistachios in a bowl and toss to combine. Set aside.

Preheat a chargrill pan or barbecue to medium-high heat.

Grill the burgers for 4–5 minutes each side until cooked through. Spread the base of each bread roll with the harissa mayonnaise. Add the lamb burger, then top with the orange relish and micro salad leaves and serve. **Makes 4**

* Micro salad leaves are from farmers' markets and selected greengrocers. Harissa (a North African chilli paste) and slivered pistachios are from gourmet food shops.

Dukkah-crusted lamb with radish tzatziki

1 tbs pomegranate molasses*, plus extra to drizzle
1 tbs honey, warmed
1 cup dukkah*
12 French-trimmed lamb cutlets
1 tbs olive oil
6 radishes, trimmed
1 telegraph cucumber
250g thick Greek-style yoghurt
2 garlic cloves, crushed
2 tbs chopped mint, plus leaves to garnish
Seeds of 1 pomegranate* (optional), to garnish

Preheat the oven to 180°C.

Combine the pomegrante molasses and honey in a bowl, and spread the dukkah in a separate shallow bowl.

Season the cutlets with salt and pepper. Heat the oil in a frypan over medium-high heat and cook the cutlets, in 2 batches, for 1 minute each side until sealed. Brush the cutlets with the molasses mixture, then dip in the dukkah to coat. Place on a lined baking tray and cook in the oven for a further 5 minutes until cooked but still pink in the centre.

Meanwhile, to make the tzatziki, coarsely grate the radishes and cucumber. Transfer to a sieve and squeeze out excess moisture. Combine with the yoghurt, garlic and mint, then season with salt and pepper.

Drizzle the extra pomegranate molasses over the cutlets and garnish with the pomegranate seeds. Serve with the tzatziki, garnished with the mint leaves. **Serves 4**

* Pomegranate molasses and dukkah (a spice, nut and seed blend) are from Middle Eastern shops and delis. Pomegranates are available in season from greengrocers.

Lamb and kumara tagine

1 tbs olive oil

6 x 100g lamb chump chops

1 onion, thinly sliced

2cm piece ginger, grated

4 garlic cloves, finely
   chopped

1 tbs ras el hanout*

1 tbs harissa*

1 bunch coriander, roots and
   stems finely chopped,
   leaves reserved for
   couscous

400g can chopped tomatoes

800g kumara, chopped

2 tbs lemon juice

1 tbs soy sauce

2 tbs honey

2 cinnamon quills

2 cups (500ml) beef stock

Pomegranate couscous

1 cup (200g) couscous

1 tsp harissa*

1 tbs pomegranate molasses*

1 tsp ras el hanout*

Juice of ½ lemon

1 small red onion, thinly
   sliced

Seeds of 1 pomegranate*

Preheat the oven to 180°C.

Place the oil in a flameproof casserole over medium-high heat. Season the lamb chops and cook, in batches, for 2–3 minutes each side until browned. Remove from the pan and set aside.

Add the onion to the pan and cook, stirring, for 1–2 minutes until soft. Add the ginger, garlic, ras el hanout, harissa and coriander root and stem, then cook, stirring, for 1 minute or until fragrant. Return the lamb chops to the pan with the tomatoes, kumara, lemon juice, soy sauce, honey and cinnamon, stirring to combine. Add the stock and bring to a simmer, then cover and transfer to the oven to bake for 2 hours or until the meat is falling off the bone.

Meanwhile, for the couscous, place the couscous in a bowl with the harissa, pomegranate molasses and ras el hanout, stirring to combine. Pour in 400ml boiling water, then cover and stand for 5 minutes or until the water has been absorbed. Fluff with a fork, then toss with the remaining ingredients and the reserved coriander leaves.

Serve the tagine with the couscous. **Serves 6**

* Ras el hanout (a Middle Eastern spice mix), harissa (a North African chilli paste) and pomegranate molasses are from Middle Eastern food shops. Pomegranates are available in season from greengrocers.

Sukiyaki beef with edamame and sushi rice

200g podded frozen
    edamame (soy beans)*
1 tbs olive oil
4 x 180g beef eye fillet steaks
3cm piece ginger, thinly
    sliced
3 small red chillies, seeds
    removed, thinly sliced
2 tbs dark soy sauce
2 tbs sake
2 tbs mirin (Japanese rice
    wine)*
Shredded spring onions, to
    garnish
Wasabi paste*, to serve

Sushi rice
1½ cups (300g) sushi rice
2½ tbs caster sugar
¼ cup (60ml) rice vinegar

For the sushi rice, wash the rice under cold water until the water runs clear. Place in a saucepan with 450ml water, cover and slowly bring to the boil. Boil for 3 minutes, then reduce the heat to low and cook for 9 minutes. Remove from the heat and stand, covered, for 10 minutes until the rice is tender. Meanwhile, place the sugar and vinegar in a saucepan with 1 tsp salt and bring to the boil. Cool slightly, then stir into the rice.

Cook the edamame in boiling, salted water for 5 minutes until tender, then drain. Keep warm.

Heat the oil in a large frypan over medium-high heat. Season the steaks, then cook, turning to seal on all sides, for 5 minutes. Cover loosely with foil and set aside while you make the sauce.

Return the frypan to medium-high heat, add the ginger and chilli and cook for 1–2 minutes until softened. Add the soy sauce, sake and mirin and cook, stirring, until thick and sticky. Cut each steak into cubes, then reassemble on the rice. Pour over the sauce, scatter with the edamame and spring onion, then serve with the wasabi. **Serves 4**

* From Asian food shops and selected supermarkets.

Pea felafel with pita and herby yoghurt

2 tsp cumin seeds

2 tsp coriander seeds

½ cup (100g) dried split
   green peas

1½ cups (180g) frozen peas,
   thawed

1 tbs grated lemon zest

1 tbs lemon juice

½ tsp baking powder

1 tbs plain flour

¼ tsp chilli powder

2 garlic cloves, roughly
   chopped

2 tbs chopped flat-leaf
   parsley leaves

⅓ cup (80ml) sunflower oil,
   to shallow-fry

4 small pita bread, grilled or
   warmed

Lemon wedges, to serve

Herby yoghurt

100ml thick Greek-style
   yoghurt

1 tbs chopped coriander
   leaves

1 tbs chopped mint leaves,
   plus extra leaves to serve

Squeeze of lime or lemon
   juice

Toast the cumin and coriander seeds in a dry frypan over medium heat for 30 seconds or until fragrant. Crush the seeds with the dried split peas in a spice grinder or mortar and pestle to a fine powder, then place in a food processor with the thawed peas. Add the lemon zest and juice, baking powder, flour, chilli powder, garlic and parsley, then pulse to a coarse paste. Using damp hands, mould the mixture into 12 felafel balls. Chill for 15 minutes or until firm.

Meanwhile, for the herby yoghurt, combine the ingredients in a bowl, then set aside.

Preheat the oven to 170°C. Heat 2cm oil in a non-stick frypan over medium-high heat. In 2 batches, fry the felafel for 4 minutes, turning, until crisp and golden all over. Keep the first batch warm in a low oven while you cook the remaining felafel.

Serve the felafel with the grilled pita, herby yoghurt, lemon wedges and extra mint leaves. **Serves 4**

Anglo-Indian eggs

8 eggs

1 tbs canola oil

1 large onion, thinly sliced

10–12 fresh curry leaves*

1 tbs panch phora*

2–3 tbs mild curry powder

200ml ready-made
hollandaise sauce*

200ml pure (thin) cream

270ml can coconut milk

¼ cup (60ml) lemon juice

Steamed basmati rice and
naan bread, to serve

Coriander leaves, to garnish

Place the eggs in a saucepan and cover with plenty of cold water. Bring to the boil, then reduce heat to medium and simmer for 6 minutes until hard-boiled. Refresh the eggs under cold water and peel when cool enough to handle. Halve the eggs and set aside.

Heat the oil in a heavy-based saucepan over medium heat. Add the onion and cook for 3–5 minutes until softened. Add the curry leaves and panch phora and cook, stirring, for 1 minute until fragrant. Stir in the curry powder and cook for a further 1 minute until fragrant. Add the hollandaise, cream and coconut milk and simmer over low heat for 2–3 minutes. Season with salt and pepper, then add the lemon juice and halved eggs and warm through.

Spoon the eggs and sauce onto the steamed rice, garnish with the coriander leaves and serve with the naan bread. **Serves 4**

* Fresh curry leaves are from greengrocers and Indian food shops. Panch phora (a mix of whole spices including cumin, fennel, fenugreek, mustard and nigella seeds) is from Indian and gourmet food shops. Hollandaise sauce is from supermarkets.

Moroccan carrot and chickpea stew

2 tbs olive oil

1 onion, thinly sliced

3 garlic cloves, finely
chopped

½ tsp each ground coriander,
cumin, turmeric, ginger,
cayenne pepper and
paprika

2 bunches baby (Dutch)
carrots, peeled, ends
trimmed with some stem
left intact

1 parsnip, peeled, cut into
batons

400g can chopped tomatoes

2 tbs lemon juice

1 cup (250ml) vegetable stock
or water

400g can chickpeas, drained,
rinsed

⅓ cup chopped coriander
leaves

2 tsp chopped mint leaves

Couscous, to serve

Heat the oil in a large saucepan over medium heat. Add the onion
and cook, stirring, for 2 minutes or until starting to soften. Add the
garlic and spices and stir for a few seconds until fragrant, then add
the carrots and parsnip and stir to coat in the spices. Stir in the
tomatoes, lemon juice and stock or water, then cover and simmer
for about 20 minutes or until the vegetables are tender. Add the
chickpeas and heat through for 2–3 minutes. Remove from the heat,
then stir through the coriander and mint. Serve with the couscous.
Serves 4

Son-in-law eggs

2 eggs
3 cups (750ml) vegetable oil
1 butter lettuce, outer leaves
   discarded, leaves
   separated
2 large vine-ripened
   tomatoes, quartered
1 spring onion, very thinly
   sliced
1 long red chilli, thinly sliced
   on an angle
Fried Asian shallots* and
   chopped toasted peanuts,
   to garnish
2 tbs oyster sauce

Break the eggs into 2 separate cups. Heat the oil in a wok or saucepan over high heat. Just before the oil starts to smoke, carefully slide the eggs, one at a time, into the oil and fry for 1 minute, basting and turning with a long metal spoon (be careful, as the oil will spit slightly), until the white is crisp and cooked – the yolk will still be a little runny.

Use a slotted spoon to remove the eggs from the oil, then place on paper towel to drain.

Place the lettuce leaves on 2 serving plates. Place an egg in each lettuce cup with some of the tomato. Top with the onion and chilli and garnish with the fried shallots and peanuts. Drizzle over the oyster sauce. **Serves 2**

* Fried Asian shallots are from Asian food shops and selected supermarkets.

Moroccan pasta

2 tbs olive oil

1 onion, finely chopped

2 garlic cloves, finely
   chopped

1 tsp ground cinnamon

1 tsp ground cumin

¼ tsp ground turmeric

½ tsp sweet paprika

400g can chopped tomatoes

½ cup (125ml) chicken
   or vegetable stock

400g can chickpeas, rinsed,
   drained

400g small pasta shapes
   (such as orecchiette or
   penne)

1 cup each mint, parsley and
   coriander leaves, plus extra
   to serve

100g pine nuts, toasted

Persian (marinated) feta*,
   to crumble

Sumac* and lemon wedges,
   to serve

Heat the olive oil in a frypan over medium heat, then add the onion and garlic and cook, stirring, for 3–4 minutes until softened. Add the spices and cook for 30 seconds until fragrant, then add the canned tomatoes and stock or water, and simmer over medium-low heat for 10 minutes. Add the chickpeas and stir for 1–2 minutes until heated through.

Meanwhile, cook the pasta according to the packet instructions. Drain, then add to the pan of sauce with the fresh herbs. Season well, then toss over low heat until combined.

Place the pasta in a large serving bowl, then scatter with the pine nuts, extra herbs, feta and sumac. Serve with the lemon wedges to squeeze over. **Serves 4**

* Persian feta and sumac (a lemony Middle Eastern spice made from ground dried berries) are from supermarkets.

White bean and coconut curry

2 tbs sunflower oil
1 tsp yellow mustard seeds
12 fresh curry leaves*
1 onion, thinly sliced
2cm piece ginger, grated
4 garlic cloves, finely
   chopped
3 tsp mild curry powder
4 cardamom pods, lightly
   bruised
½ tsp ground turmeric
½ tsp chilli powder
1 tsp ground coriander
⅔ cup (165ml) coconut milk
2 x 400g cans cannellini
   beans, rinsed, drained
250g punnet cherry or grape
   tomatoes, halved
2 tsp sugar
Juice of 1 lime
2 tbs chopped coriander
   leaves, plus extra leaves to
   garnish
Steamed basmati rice and
   naan bread, to serve

Heat the oil in a large saucepan over medium-low heat. Add the mustard seeds and cook for 30 seconds or until they start to pop. Add the curry leaves and onion and cook, stirring, for 3–5 minutes until the onion has softened.

   Add the ginger, garlic, curry powder, cardamom and dry spices and cook, stirring, for 1–2 minutes until fragrant. Add the coconut milk and 200ml water and bring to a simmer. Reduce the heat to low and simmer for 3–5 minutes until slightly thickened. Add the beans, tomato, sugar and lime juice and simmer for a further 2–3 minutes until the tomato has softened slightly. Stir through the chopped coriander leaves. Serve with the rice and naan, garnished with extra coriander leaves. **Serves 4**

* From selected greengrocers.

Index